The Mind as Nature

THE JOHN DEWEY SOCIETY LECTURESHIP SERIES

The John Dewey Society Lecture is delivered annually under the sponsorship of the John Dewey Society at the annual meeting of the National Society of College Teachers of Education. Arrangements for the presentation and publication of the Lecture are under the direction of the John Dewey Society Commission on Publications.

ARTHUR G. WIRTH, Washington University, St. Louis, Missouri
Chairman and Editor

The John Dewey Society Lectureship——Number Five

THE MIND
AS NATURE

by

Loren Eiseley

Foreword by

ARTHUR G. WIRTH

Chairman, The John Dewey Society
Commission on Publications

HARPER & ROW, PUBLISHERS
NEW YORK, EVANSTON
AND LONDON

Library of Congress catalog card number: 62-14589

For
Letta May Clark
Former Supervisor of English, University of Nebraska
High School
In gratitude for counsel and encouragement
in my youth

Foreword

by Arthur G. Wirth, Chairman, *The John Dewey Society Commission on Publications*

In *The Mind as Nature* we are presented with an analysis of a drama in which the whole of nature as well as each of us are actors in the basic plot. At issue is the process of creativity seeking to realize itself. The protagonists constitute, on the one hand, all that is involved in the creative potential to bring forth new forms and, on the other, all that inhibits the novel and fresh which might come into being.

The drama is played out at many levels. The biosphere itself provides the nurture for life in its marvelous and varied forms, yet it also functions in ways to block or choke diverse modes which might have been. Human culture is an indispensable storehouse for sustaining and furthering growth of the human spirit, but it may function also an an agent for atrophy. The peculiarities of our own individual histories similarly may

7

provide access to resources that free us to produce, or close us off from, the rich and varied paths we might have opened for ourselves.

Since the special concern of the essay is for the process of teaching, Dr. Eiseley points out that the teacher is part of the universal drama and plays, in fact, a peculiarly critical role. In the vivid phrase of the author, "The educator can be the withholder as well as the giver of life." By understanding this properly we are led to see that the whole process of contemporary education is shot through with possibilities of action that can free the processes of growth in our students, or can cripple and stunt them.

In his reflections on the nature of creativity, Dr. Eiseley, for example, explores the histories of men of genius for clues as to sources of their productivity. While this is a fascinating chapter in itself, he reminds us of vital consequences for the act of teaching. One important facet of teaching that may liberate young minds is to make available the illuminating insights of trail-blazing thinkers. The true teacher knows, however, that this potentially exciting process may degenerate into dull and sterile repetition. To help his students sense the quality of the insights involved, the teacher-scholar will realize the need to immerse himself in the meaning-giving ideas so that he has shared fully in the luminosity they provide.

We are reminded, too, that the very size and efficiency of the modern educational enterprise may pose special threats. As our mechanisms for processing students become more elaborate; as we categorize, sort and tabulate with greater confidence, we may succeed in cutting ourselves off from the inner life of students where the factors of growth move in their subtle and often wayward paths that will not always mesh with the clicking IBM cards.

The teaching profession must be on guard against the manifold anxieties and pressures of the social system that work to restrict the opportunities for human learning. At the same time teachers must realize that their own inner angers and personal rigidities may affect their relations with students so as to close doors to avenues of exploration which might have been made available.

There is the possibility, too, that with all of our efforts to understand creativity we may explain it away by an overly compulsive analysis. The process itself contains the elements of indeterminacy and contingency. Only by establishing an open-ended society and a flexible imagination that can accommodate the unpredictable will we have done our necessary part.

While this study reveals the complex of events involved in creativity, the reader may wish to consider to what extent the essay itself is a demonstration of the creative process. We refer here to a summary description of creative individuals that has emerged from six years of intensive research on the subject:

... What seems to characterize the creative person—and this is especially so for the artistically creative—is a relative absence of repression and suppression as mechanisms for the control of impulse and imagery. Repression operates against creativity, regardless of how intelligent a person may be, because it makes unavailable to the individual large aspects of his own experience. . . . Disassociated items of experience cannot combine with one another; there are barriers to communication among different systems of experience. The creative person, given to expression rather than suppression or repression, thus has fuller access to his own experience, both conscious and unconscious. Furthermore, because the unconscious operates more by symbols than by logic, the creative person is more open to the perception of complex equivalences in experience, facility in metaphor being one specific consequence of the creative person's greater openness to his own depth.*

This lecture comes at a moment when we are stirred by man's first efforts to explore the space beyond his earth. We sense in such events that man stands on the thresh-

* Donald W. M. MacKinnon, "What Makes a Person Creative," *Saturday Review*, February 10, 1962, pp. 15 ff. A report by the director of the Institute of Personality Assessment and Research at the University of California in Berkeley.

10

hold of a new and uncharted chapter in his history. We are confronted again with the urgent and perennial questions: What is Man? What might he become? Loren Eiseley through the years has kept questions like these at the center of his attention. His capacity to combine the insights of science, the humanities, and philosophy equips him in an unusual way to provide a saving perspective—a kind of perspective that becomes more urgent as our specialization makes it more difficult to maintain meaningful communciation, and to see the large questions of human import with wholeness.

As a scientist Dr. Eiseley's general concern has been with the evolution of life—but more specifically with the emergence of the human experience. He has roamed the western regions of this American continent to find clues of the earliest human life here and has published widely in the technical journals of his discipline.

As a poet and writer he has been a contributor to leading literary anthologies as well as to such magazines as *Saturday Evening Post, Saturday Review, Harper's Magazine, Scientific American,* and *Reader's Digest* as well as to the *New York Times* and the *New York Herald Tribune.*

His philosophical perspective is evidenced by his being commissioned by the American Philosophical

11

Society for studies involving the Darwin Centennial and the 400th Anniversary of Francis Bacon.

In recent years he has served as provost of the University of Pennsylvania and chairman of the Department of Anthropology. He is now University Professor of Anthropology and the History of Science and chairman of the Department of History and Philosophy of Science in the Graduate School at the University of Pennsylvania.

Dr. Eiseley has reached his most extensive audience through his widely admired books: *The Immense Journey, Darwin's Century* and *The Firmament of Time. The Mind as Nature* was completed while the author was in residence at The Institute for Advanced Study in the Behavioral Sciences, Stanford, California.

The present volume is the fifth in the annual John Dewey Series and represents one part of the program of publications of The John Dewey Society for the Study of Education and Culture. In the series the society seeks to provide a forum for leading thinkers from various fields of the intellectual life of America in which they can examine questions involved in the relations of education and culture. The lecture is presented each year in Chicago as a cooperative venture of The John Dewey Society and The National Society for College Teachers of Education.

"Divine imaginings, like gods, come down to the groves of our Thessalies, and there, in the embrace of wild, dryad reminiscences, beget the beings that astonish the world."
—Herman Melville, *Redburn*

"To imagine is an act which gives human beings the chance to engage in something akin to creation."
—René Dubos, *The Dreams of Reason*

The Mind as Nature

When I was a small boy I lived, more than most children, in two worlds. One was dark, hidden and self-examining, though in its own way not without compensations. The other world in which I somehow also managed to exist was external, boisterous, and what I suppose the average parent would call normal or extroverted. These two worlds simultaneously existing in one growing brain had in them something of the dichotomy present in the actual universe where one finds behind the ridiculous, wonderful tentshow of woodpeckers, giraffes, and hoptoads, some kind of dark, brooding, but creative void out of which these things emerge—some anti-matter universe, some web of dark tensions running beneath and creating the superficial show of form that so delights us. If I develop this little story of a personal experience as a kind of parable, it is because I believe that in one way or another we mirror in ourselves the universe with all its dark vacuity and also its simultane-

17

ous urge to create anew, in each generation, the beauty and the terror of our mortal existence.

In my own case, through the accidents of fortune, the disparity between these two worlds was vastly heightened. Why I managed to exist in both I do not know. Children under such disharmony often grow sick, retire inward, choose to return to the void. I have known such cases. I am not unaware that I paid a certain price for my survival and indeed have been paying for it ever since. Yet the curious thing is that I survived and, looking back, I have a growing feeling that the experience was good for me. I think I learned something from it even while I passed through certain humiliations and an utter and profound loneliness. I was living, you see, in a primitive world at the same time that I was inhabiting the modern world as it existed in the second decade of this century. I am not talking now about the tree-house, cave-building activities of normal boys. I am talking about the minds of the first dawning human consciousness—about a kind of mental Ice Age, and of how a light came in from outside until, as I have indicated, two worlds existed in which a boy, still a single unsplit personality, walked readily from one world to the other by day and by night without anyone observing the invisible boundaries he passed.

I

To begin this story I have to strip myself of certain conventions, but since all the major figures of my childhood are dead I can harm no one but myself. I think, if we are to find our way into the nature of creativeness, into those multitudinous universes that inhabit the minds of men, such case histories—though I hate this demeaning term—have a certain value. Perhaps if we were franker on these matters with our students, we might reach out and occasionally touch, with a passing radiance, some other star in the night.

I was born in the first decade of this century, conceived in, and part of the rolling yellow cloud that occasionally raises up a rainy silver eye to look upon itself before subsiding into dust again. That cloud has been blowing in my part of the Middle West since the Ice Age. Only a few months ago, flying across the continent, I knew we were passing over it in its customary place. It was still there and its taste was still upon my tongue.

In those days I lived like most American boys of that section, in a small house where the uncemented cellar occasionally filled with water and the parlor was kept shuttered in a perpetual cool darkness. We never

19

had visitors. No minister ever called on us, so the curtains were never raised. We were, in a sense, social outcasts. We were not bad people nor did we belong to a racial minority. We were simply shunned as unimportant and odd.

The neighbors were justified in this view. My mother was stone deaf, my father worked the long hours of a time when labor was still labor. I was growing up alone in a house whose dead silence was broken only by the harsh discordant jangling of a voice that could not hear itself. My mother had lost her hearing as a young girl. I never learned what had attracted my father to her. I never learned by what fantastic chance I had come to exist at all. Only the cloud would know, I sometimes think to this day, only the yellow loess cloud rolling, impenetrable as it was when our ancestors first emerged from it on the Ice Age steppes of Europe, or when they followed the bison into its heart on the wide American plains.

I turned over the bricks of our front sidewalk and watched ants with a vague interest. There grew up between my mother and myself an improvised system of communication consisting of hand signals, stampings on the floor to create vibrations, exaggerated lip movements vaguely reminiscent of an anthropoid society.

We did not consciously work at this. We were far too ignorant. Certain acts were merely found useful and came to be repeated and to take on symbolic value. It was something of the kind of communication which may have been conducted by the man apes of the early Ice Age. One might say we were at the speech threshold— not much more.

I did not go to church, and since the family was not agreed upon any mode of worship, I merely wondered as I grew older how it was that things came to be. In short, I would have been diagnosed today by social workers as a person suffering from societal deprivation and headed for trouble.

There was another curious aspect of this family which involved my father. He was a good man who bore the asperities of my afflicted mother with dignity and restraint. He had been a strolling itinerant actor in his younger years, a largely self-trained member of one of those little troupes who played *East Lynne* and declaimed raw Shakespearean melodrama to unsophisticated audiences in the little Midwestern "opera houses." He had a beautiful resonant speaking voice. Although we owned no books, and although when I knew him in middle age a harsh life had dimmed every hunger except that for rest, he could still declaim long rolling Eliza-

21

bethan passages that caused shivers to run up my back.

> Put on my robes, give me my crown, I have
> immortal longings in me.

Like many failures of his time he used to speak wistfully of cheap land in Arkansas and send for catalogues, searching for something that was permanently lost. It was the last of the dream that had finally perished under the yellow cloud. I write the word "failure" in a worldly sense only. He was not a failure as a man. He reared a son, the product of an unfortunate marriage from which he might easily have fled, leaving me inarticulate. He was kind and thoughtful with an innate courtesy that no school in that rough land had taught him. Although he was intensely sensitive, I saw him weep but twice. The first time, when I was young and very ill, I looked up in astonishment as a tear splashed on my hand. The second time, long years afterward, belongs to him and his life alone. I will merely say he had had a great genius for love and that his luck was very bad. He was not fitted for life under the yellow cloud. He knew it, yet played out his role there to the end. So poor were we, it took me twenty years to put a monument upon his grave.

II

We come now to the two worlds of which I spoke, and which I said constitute a parable, a personal exploration of the subject of this lecture and its relation to John Dewey: the two worlds making up the mind and heart of this curiously deprived and solitary child—a child whose mother's speech was negligible and disordered and which left him for the greater part of his young childhood involved with only rudimentary communication and the conscious rebuffs of neighbors; or another ill-understood world of haunting grandiloquent words at which his playmates laughed; or even a third world where he sat, the last little boy, and watched the great green moths beat past under the street lamps.

Into what well of being does one then descend for strength? How does one choose one's life? Or does one just go on without guidance as in a dark town, from one spot of light to the next? "Uncertainty," as John Dewey has well said, "is primarily a practical matter." It signifies uncertainty of the *issue* of present experiences. These are fraught with future peril. . . . The intrinsic troublesome and uncertain quality of situations lies in the fact that they hold outcomes in suspense; they move to evil or to good fortune. The natural tendency of man is to do something at once, there is impatience with suspense, and lust for immediate action."

It is here amid a chaos of complexities that the teacher, frequently with blindness, with uncertainties of his own, must fight with circumstance for the developing mind—perhaps even for the very survival of the child. The issue cannot be long delayed because, as Dewey observes, man—and far more, the child—has a lust for the immediate, for action. Yet the teacher is fighting for an oncoming future, for something that has not emerged, which may, in fact, never emerge. His lot is worse than that of the sculptors in snow, which Sydney Hook once described us as being. Rather, the teacher is a sculptor of the intangible future. There is no more dangerous occupation on the planet, for what we conceive as our masterpiece may appear out of time to mock us—a horrible caricature of ourselves.

The teacher must ever walk warily between the necessity of inducing those conformities which in every generation reaffirm our rebellious humanity, yet he must at the same time allow for the free play of the creative spirit. It is not only for the sake of the future that the true educator fights, it is for the justification of himself, his profession, and the state of his own soul. He, too, amid contingencies and weariness, without mental an-

24

tennae, and with tests that fail him, is a savior of souls. He is giving shapes to time, and the shapes themselves, driven by their own inner violence, wrench free of his control—must, if they are truly sculptured, surge like released genii from the classroom or, tragically, shrink to something less than bottle size.

The teacher cannot create, any more than can the sculptor, the stone upon which he exercises his talents; he cannot, it is true, promote gene changes and substitutions in the bodies with which he works. But here again Dewey has words of peculiar pertinence to us—words which remove from the genes something of the utter determinacy in which the geneticist sometimes revels. "In the continuous ongoing of life," contends the philosopher, "objects part with something of their final character and become conditions of subsequent experiences. There is regulation of the change in which . . . a causal character is rendered preparatory and instrumental." The boy under the street lamp may become fascinated by night-flying moths or the delinquent whisperings of companions. Or he may lie awake in the moonlight of his room, quaking with the insecurity of a divided household and the terrors of oncoming adulthood. He may quietly continue some lost part of childhood by playing immense and solitary games with toys he would not dare

25

to introduce among his raucous companions of the street. He wanders forlornly through a museum and is impressed by a kindly scientist engrossed in studying some huge bones.

Objects do indeed "part with something of their final character" and so do those who teach. There are subjects in which I have remained dwarfed all of my adult life because of the ill-considered blow of someone nursing pent-up aggressions, or words more violent in their end effects than blows. There are other subjects for which I have more than ordinary affection because they are associated in my mind with kindly and understanding men or women—sculptors who left even upon such impliant clay as mine the delicate chiseling of refined genius, who gave unwittingly, in other words, something of their final character to most unpromising material. Sculptors reaching blindly forward into time, they struck out their creation scarce living to view the result.

Now, for many years an educator, I often feel the need to seek out a quiet park bench to survey mentally that vast and nameless river of students which has poured under my hands. In pain I have meditated: "This man is dead—a suicide. Was it I, all unknowingly, who directed, in some black hour, his hand upon the gun?" "This man is a liar and a cheat. Where did my stroke go wrong?" Or there comes to memory the man who, after long endeavors, returned happily to the farm from which he had come. Did I serve him, if not in the world's eye, well? Or the richly endowed young poet whom I sheltered from his father's wrath—was I pampering or defending—and at the right or the wrong moment in his life? Contingency, contingency, and each day by word or deed the chisel falling true or blind upon the future of some boy or girl.

Ours is an ill-paid profession and we have our share of fools. We, too, like the generation before us, are the cracked, the battered, the malformed products of remoter chisels shaping the most obstinate substance in the universe: the substance of man. Someone has to do it, but perhaps it might be done more kindly, more precisely, to the extent that we are consciously aware of what we do—even if that thought sometimes congeals our hearts with terror. Or, if we were more conscious of our task, would our hands shake or grow immobilized upon the chisel?

I do not know. I know only that in these late fainthearted years I sometimes pause with my hand upon the knob before I go forth into the classroom. I am afflicted in this fashion because I have come to follow Dewey in his remarks that "nature is seen to be marked by histories." As an evolutionist I am familiar with that vast sprawling emergent, the universe, and its even more fantastic shadow, life. Stranger still, however, is the record of the artist who creates the symbols by which we live. As Dewey has again anticipated, "No mechanically exact science of an individual is possible. An individual is a history unique in character." "But," he remarks, "constitutents of an individual are known when they are regarded not as qualitative, but as statistical constants derived from a series of operations."

I should like shortly to survey a few such constants from the lives of certain great literary figures with whose works I happen to be reasonably familiar. I choose to do so because creativity—that enigma to which the modern student of educational psychology is devoting more and more attention—is particularly "set in the invisible." "The tangible," Dewey insisted in *Experience and Nature* "rests precariously upon the untouched and ungrasped." Dewey abhorred the inculcation of fixed conclusions at the expense of man's originality. Though my case histories are neither numerous nor similar, we shall observe in them certain constants that, without revealing the total nature of genius, throw light upon the odd landscapes and interiors which have nurtured it.

III

"A person too early cut off from the common interests of men," Jean Rostand, the French biologist, recently remarked, "is exposed to inner impoverishment. Like those islands which are lacking in some whole class of mammals." Naturally there are degrees of such isolation, but I would venture the observation that this eminent observer has overlooked one thing: sometimes on such desert islands there has been a great evolutionary proliferation amongst the flora and fauna that remain. Strange shapes, exotic growths which, on the mainland, would have been quickly strangled by formidable enemies, here spring up readily. Sometimes the rare, the beautiful can only emerge or survive in isolation. In a similar manner, some degree of withdrawal serves to nurture man's creative powers. The artist and scientist bring out of the dark void, like the mysterious universe itself, the unique, the strange, the unexpected. Numerous late observers have testified upon the loneliness of the process.

"The whole of my pleasure," wrote Darwin of his travels with illiterate companions on the high Andean uplands, "was derived from what passed in my mind." The mind, in other words, has a latent, lurking fertility, not unrelated to the universe from which it sprang. Even in want and in jail it will labor, and if it does not produce a physical escape, it will appear, assuming the motivational drive be great enough, in *Pilgrim's Progress,* that still enormously moving account of one who walked through the wilderness of this world, and laid him down and dreamed a dream. That dream, as John Bunyan himself wrote, "will make a Traveller of Thee." It was the account of the journey from the City of Destruction to the City of God. It was written by a man in homespun not even aware of being a conscious artist, nor interested in personal fame. Three centuries later he would be better known than many kings.

The fact is that many of us who walk to and fro upon our usual tasks are prisoners drawing mental maps of escape. I once knew a brilliant and discerning philosopher who spent many hours each week alone in movie houses watching indifferently pictures of a quality far below his actual intellectual tastes. I knew him as an able, friendly, and normal person. Somewhere behind this sunny mask, however, he was in flight, from what, I never knew. Was it job, home, family—or was it rather something lost that he was seeking? Whatever it was, the pictures that passed before his eyes, the sounds, only half-heard, could have meant little except for an occasional face, a voice, a fading bar of music. No, it was the darkness and the isolation he wanted, something in the deep night of himself that called him home.

The silver screen was only a doorway to a land he had entered long ago. It was weirdly like hashish or opium. He taught well, he was far better read than many who climbed to national reputation upon fewer abilities than he possessed. His kindness to others was proverbial, his advice the sanest a friend could give. Only the pen was denied to him and so he passed toward his end, leaving behind the quick streak of a falling star that slips from sight. A genius in personal relationships, he was voiceless—somewhere a door had been softly, courteously, but inexorably closed within his brain. It would never open again within his lifetime.

I knew another man of similar capacities—a scholar who had shifted in his last graduate days from the field of the classics to the intricacies of zoology. A scintillating piece of research had rocked his profession, and he had marched steadily to the headship of a great department. He, too, was a graying, handsome man, with the world at his feet. He did not fail in health, his students loved him, and he loved them. The research died. This happens to other men. His problem was more serious: he could not answer letters. His best pupils could not depend upon

31

him even to recommend them for posts or scholarships. Airmail letters lay unopened in his box. It was not that he was cruel. Anything a man could do by word of mouth he would do for his students, even if it meant the assumption of unpleasant tasks. Firm, upright, with a grave old-fashioned gallantry, in him also a door had closed forever. One never heard him speak of his family. Somewhere behind that door was a landscape we were never permitted to enter.

One can also read case histories. There is, for example, the brilliant child who had lost a parent and then a guardian abroad. Here, in some strange transmutation, arose a keen cartographer, a map maker, seeking a way back to the lost—a student of continents, time tables, odd towns, and fading roads. This is a juvenile case and the end, therefore, uncertain. One wonders whether there will come a breaking point where, as eventually they must, the trails within dissolve to waving grass and the crossroad signs lie twisted and askew on rotting posts. Where, then, will the wanderer turn? Will the last sign guide him safely home at last—or will he become one of the dawdlers, the evaders, unconscious fighters of some cruel inner master. It is of great interest in this connection that Herman Melville, who had lost his father under painful circumstances in his youth, describes in *Redburn,* in fictional guise, what must have lain close to his own heart: the following of a thirty-year-old map which traced the wanderings of Redburn's father in Liverpool. These passages are handled with the kind of imaginative power that indicates Melville's deep personal involvement in this aspect of Redburn's story. He speaks of running in the hope of overtaking the lost father at the next street, then the map fails him, just as the father himself had gone where no son's search could find him. Again in *Moby Dick* he cries out "Where is the foundling's father hidden?" I think of my own slow journeys homeward from one arc light to another in a city whose name now comes with difficulty to my tongue.

In some of us a child—lost, strayed off the beaten path—goes wandering to the end of time while we, in another garb, grow up, marry or seduce, have children, hold jobs, or sit in movies, and refuse to answer our mail. Or, by contrast, we haunt our mailboxes, impelled by some strange anticipation of a message that will never come. "A man," Thoreau commented, "needs only to be turned around once with his eyes shut in this world to be lost."

But now an odd thing happens. Some of these men with maps in their heads do not remain mute. Instead, they develop the power to draw the outside world within

33

and lose us there. Or, as scientists, after some deep inner colloquy, they venture even to remake reality.

What would the modern chronicler of the lives of Hollywood celebrities feel if he were told he had to produce a great autobiography out of a year spent in a shack by a little pond, seeing scarcely anyone? Yet Henry David Thoreau did just that, and in entering what was essentially an inner forest, he influenced the lives of thousands of people all over the world and, it would appear, through succeeding generations.

There was another man, Nathaniel Hawthorne, who, as he puts it, "sat down by the wayside of life, like a man under enchantment." For over a decade he wrote in a room in Salem, subsisting on a small income, and scarcely going out before evening. "I am surrounding myself with shadows," he wrote, "which bewilder me by aping the realities of life." He found in the human heart "a terrible gloom, and monsters of diverse kinds . . . but deeper still . . . the eternal beauty." This region of guttering candles, ungainly night birds, "fragments of a world," are an interior geography through which even the modern callous reader ventures with awe.

One could run through other great creative land-scapes in the literary field. One could move with Hudson over the vast Patagonian landscape which haunted him even in his long English exile. One could, in fact, devise an anthology in which, out of the same natural background, under the same stars, beneath the same forests, or upon the same seas, each man would evoke such smoky figures from his own heart, such individual sunlight and shadow as would be his alone. St. Exupéry has his own flyer's vision of the little South American towns, or of the Andes when flying was still young. Or Herman Melville, whose Pacific was "a Potters Field of all four continents . . . mixed shades and shadows, drowned dreams, somnambulisms, reveries."

Or, to change scene into the city-world, there is the vision of London in Arthur Machen's *Hill of Dreams:* "one grey temple of an awful rite, ring within ring of wizard stones circled about some central place, every circle was an initiation, every initiation eternal loss." Perhaps it should not go unnoticed in this tale of solitude in a great city that Machen dwells upon the hatred of the average man for the artist, "a deep instinctive dread of all that was strange, uncanny, alien to his nature." Julian, Machen's hero, "could not gain the art of letters and he had lost the art of humanity." He was turning fatally inward as surely as those men whose stories I have recounted.

Perhaps there is a moral here which should not go

35

unobserved, and which makes the artist's problem greater. It also extends to the scientist, particularly as in the case of Darwin or Freud, or, in earlier centuries, such men as Giordano Bruno or Francis Bacon. "Humanity is not, as was once thought," says John Dewey, "the end for which all things were formed; it is but a slight and feeble thing, perhaps an episodic one, in the vast stretch of the universe. But for man, man is the center of interest and the measure of importance."

IV

It is frequently the tragedy of the great artist, as it is of the great scientist, that he frightens the ordinary man. If he is more than a popular story teller it may take humanity a generation to absorb and grow accustomed to the new geography with which scientist or artist presents us. Even then, perhaps only the more imaginative and literate may accept him. Subconsciously the genius is feared as an image breaker; frequently he does not accept the opinions of the mass, nor man's opinion of himself. He has voiced through the ages, in one form or another, this very loneliness and detachment which Dewey has seen so clearly as the outcome of our extending knowledge. The custom-bound, uneducated, intolerant man projects his fear and hatred upon the seer. The artist is frequently a human mirror. If what we see there displeases us, if we see all too clearly our own insignificance and vanity, we tend to revolt, not against ourselves, but in order to martyrize the unfortunate soul who forced us into self-examination.

In short, like the herd animals we are, we sniff warily at the strange one among us. If he is fortunate enough finally to be accepted, it is apt to be after a trial of ridicule and after the sting has been removed from his work by long familiarization and bowdlerizing, when the alien quality of his thought has been mitigated or removed. Carl Schneer recounts that Einstein made so little impression on his superiors, it was with difficulty that he obtained even a junior clerkship in the Swiss Patents office at Bern, after having failed of consideration as a scholar of promise. Not surprisingly, theoretical physicists favored his views before the experimentalists capitulated. As Schneer remarks: "It was not easy to have a twenty-six-year-old clerk in the Swiss Patents office explain the meaning of experiments on which one had labored for years." Implacable hatred, as well as praise, was to be Einstein's lot.

To an anthropologist, the social reception of invention reminds one of the manner in which a strange young male is first repulsed, then tolerated, upon the fringes of a group of howler monkeys he wishes to join. Finally, since the memories of the animals are short, he becomes familiar, is accepted, and fades into the mass. In a similar way, discoveries made by Darwin and Wallace were at first castigated and then by degrees absorbed. In the process both men experienced forms of loneliness and isolation not simply as a necessity for discovery but as a penalty for having dared to redraw the map of our outer, rather than inner, cosmos.

This fear of the upheld mirror in the hand of genius extends to the teaching profession and perhaps to the primary and secondary school teacher most of all. The teacher occupies, as we shall see a little further on, a particularly anomalous and exposed position in a society subject to rapid change, or threatened by exterior enemies. Society is never totally sure of what it wants of its educators. It wants, first of all, the inculcation of custom, tradition, and all that socializes the child into the good citizen. The demand for conformity in the lower grades is apt to be intense. The child himself, as well as the teacher, is apt to be under the surveillance of critical, if not opinionated, parents. Secondly, however, society wants the child to absorb new learning which will simultaneously benefit that society and enhance the individual's prospects of success.

Thus the teacher, in some degree, stands as interpreter and disseminator of the cultural mutations introduced by the individual genius into society. Some of the fear, the projected guilt feelings of those who do not wish to look into the mirrors held up to them by men of the Hawthorne stamp of genius, falls upon us. Moving among innovators of ideas as we do, sifting and judging them daily, something of the suspicion with which the mass of mankind still tends to regard its own cultural creators falls upon the teacher who plays a role of great significance in this process of cultural diffusion. He is, to a degree, placed in a paradoxical position. He is expected both to be the guardian of stability and the exponent of societal change. Since all persons do not accept new ideas at the same rate, it is impossible for the educator to please the entire society even if he remains abjectly servile. This is particularly true in a dynamic age.

Moreover, the true teacher has another allegiance than that to parents alone. Above all other classes in society, he is molding the future in the minds of the young. He is transmitting to them the aspirations of great thinkers of which their parents may have only the faintest notions. The teacher is often the first to discover the talented and unusual scholar. How he handles and encourages, or discourages, such a child may make all the difference in the world to that child's future—and to the world. It may be that he can induce in stubborn parents the conviction that their child is unusual and should be encouraged in his studies. If he is sufficiently judicious, he may even be able to help a child over the teetering planks of a broken home and a bad neighborhood. Like a responsible doctor, he knows that he will fail in many instances —that circumstances will destroy, or genes prove defective beyond hope. There is a limit, furthermore, to the energy of one particular man or woman in dealing individually with a growing mass of students.

It is just here, however—in our search for what we might call the able, all-purpose, success-modeled student —that I feel it so necessary not to lose sight of those darker, more uncertain, late-maturing, sometimes painfully abstracted youths who may represent the Darwins, Thoreaus, and Hawthornes of the next generation. As Dr. Carroll Newsom has recently emphasized in his admirable new book, *A University President Speaks Out*: real college education is not a four-year process; it should be lifelong. Men, moreover, mature in many ways and fashions. It is uncertain what Darwin's or Wallace's chances of passing a modern college board examination might have been.

I believe it useful, and not demeaning to our profession, to remember Melville's words in 1850, at a time when he was fighting horribly with the materials of what was to become his greatest book. The words, besides being prophetic in his case, bespeak the philosopher who looks beyond man as he is. He said: "I somehow cling to the wondrous fancy, that in all men hiddenly reside certain wondrous, occult properties—as in some plants and minerals—which by some happy but very rare accident (as bronze was discovered by the melting of the iron and brass at the burning of Corinth) may chance to be called forth here on earth."

As a teacher I know little about how these wondrous events come about, but I have seen them happen. I believe in them. I believe they are more apt to happen late in those whose background has been one of long deprivation. I believe that the good teacher should never grow indifferent to their possibility—not, at least, if there is evidence even in the face of failure in some subjects, of high motivation and intelligence in some specific field.

At the height of his creative powers, Thoreau wrote that "we should treat our minds as innocent and ingenuous children whose guardians we are—be careful what objects and what subjects we thrust on their attention. Even the facts of science may dust the mind by their dryness, unless they are in a sense effaced each morning, or rather rendered fertile by the dews of fresh and living truth. Every thought that passes through the mind helps to wear and tear it, and to deepen the ruts, which, as in the streets of Pompeii, evince how much it has been used. How many things there are concerning which we might well deliberate whether we had better know them!"

V

Now we as teachers, responsible to society, will appreciate that certain of these ancient institutions by which men live, are, however involved with human imperfection, the supporting bones of the societal body. Without them, without a certain degree of conformity and habit, society would literally cease to exist. The problem lies in sustaining the airy flight of the superior intellect above the necessary ruts it is forced to travel. As Thoreau comments, the heel of the true author wears out no road. "A thinker's weight is in his thought, not in his tread."

A direct analogy is evident in the biological domain,

42

where uncontrolled diversification at the species level would make for maladaptation to the environment. Yet without the emergence of superior or differently adapted individuals—beneficial mutations, in other words—the doorways to prolonged survival of the species would, under changing conditions, be closed. Similarly, if society sinks into the absolute rut of custom, if it refuses to accept beneficial mutations in the cultural realm, or to tolerate, if not promote, the life of genius, then its unwieldy slumbers may be its last. Worse is the fact that all we know of beauty and the delights of free untrammeled thought may sink to a few concealed sparks glimmering warily behind the foreheads of men no longer in a position to transfer these miraculous mutations to the society which gave them birth. Such repression is equivalent to placing an animal with a remarkable genetic heritage alone on a desert island. His strain will perish without issue. And so it is, in analogous ways, in oppressive societies or even in societies not consciously oppressive. It is all too easy to exist in an atmosphere of supposed free speech and yet bring such pressures to conform upon the individual that he is afraid to speak openly. I do not refer to mere political matters alone. There was a time in the American world when Thoreau's advice to "catalogue stars, those thoughts whose orbits are as rarely calculated as comets" could be set down without undergoing the scrutiny of twenty editors or publishers' readers. The observer of the fields was free as the astronomer to watch the aspect of his own interior heavens. He could even say boldly that he was "not concerned to express that kind of truth which Nature has expressed. Who knows but I may suggest some things to her?"

Our faith in science has become so great that though the open-ended and novelty-producing aspect of nature is scientifically recognized in the physics and biology of our time, there is often a reluctance to give voice to it in other than professional jargon. It has been my own experience, for example, among students, laymen, and some scientists, that to express even wonder about the universe—in other words, to benefit from some humble consideration of what we do not know, as well as marching to the constant drumbeat of what we call the age of technology—is regarded askance in some quarters. I have had the experience of being labeled by that vague word "mystic," because I have not been able to shut out wonder occasionally, when I have looked at the world. I have been lectured by at least one member of my profession who advised me to "explain myself"—words which sound for all the world like a humorless request for the self-accusations so popular in Communist lands. Although I have never disturbed the journals in my field with my off-hour compositions, there seemed to be a feeling on the part of this eminent personage that something vaguely heretical about the state of my own interior heavens demanded exposure or "confession" in a scientific journal. This man was unaware, in his tough laboratory attitude, that there was another world of pure reverie that is of at least equal importance to the human soul. Ironically, only last year Robert Hofstadter, Nobel Prize winner in physics, revealed a humility which would greatly become the lesser men of our age. "Man will never find the end of the trail," he said wistfully.

VI

Directly stated, the evolution of the entire universe—stars, elements, life, man—is a process of drawing something out of nothing, out of the utter void of non-being. The creative element in the mind of man—that latency which can conceive gods, carve statues, move the heart with the symbols of great poetry, or devise the formulas of modern physics—emerges in as mysterious a fashion as those elementary particles which leap into momentary existence in great cyclotrons, only to vanish again like infinitesimal ghosts. The reality we know in our limited lifetimes is dwarfed by the unseen potential of the abyss where science stops. In a similar way the smaller universe of the individual human brain has its lonely cometary passages, or flares suddenly like a super nova, only to subside in death while the waves of energy it has released roll on through unnumbered generations.

As the astrophysicist gazes upon the rare releases of power capable of devastating an entire solar system, so does the student of the behavioral sciences wonder at the manifestations of creative genius and consider whether the dark mechanisms that control the doorways of the human mind might be tripped open at more frequent intervals. Does genius emerge from the genes alone? Does the largely unknown chemistry of the brain contain at least part of the secret? Or is the number of potential cell connections involved? Or do we ordinary men carry it irretrievably locked within our subconscious minds?

That the *manifestations* of genius are culturally controlled we are well aware. The urban world, in all its diversity, provides a background, a cultural base, without which—whatever may be hidden in great minds— creativity would have had to seek other and more ephemeral expression or remain mute. Yet no development in art or scientific theory from the upper Stone Age onward seems to have demanded any further development in the brain of man. Mathematical theory, science, the glories of art lurked hidden as the potential seeds of the universe itself, in the minds of children rocked to sleep by cave fires in Ice Age Europe.

If genius is a purely biological phenomenon one must assume that the chances of its appearance should increase with the size of populations. Yet it is plain that, like toadstools which spring up in the night in fairy rings and then vanish, there is some delicate soil which nurtures genius—the cultural circumstance and the play of minds must meet. It is not a matter of population statistics alone, else there would not have been so surprising an efflorescence of genius in fourth- and fifth-century Greece—a thing we still marvel at in our vastly expanded world. Darwin, committed to biological explanations alone, was left fumbling uncertainly with a problem that was essentially not reducible to a simplistic biological explanation. Without ignoring the importance of biology as one aspect of an infinitely complicated subject, therefore, the modern researcher favors the view that the intensive examination of the creative mind and its environment may offer some hope of stimulating the sources from which it springs, or, at the very least, of nurturing it more carefully.

In the course of our discussion we have touched upon loneliness, the dweller in the forest as represented by Thoreau, the isolated man in the room who was Hawthorne, and those wandering recluse scientists such as Darwin and Wallace. This loneliness, in the case of literary men, frequently leads to an intense self-examination. "Who placed us with eyes between a microscopic and telescopic world?" questions Thoreau. "I have the habit of attention to such excess that my senses get no rest, but suffer from a constant strain."

Thoreau here expresses the intense self-awareness which is both the burden and delight of the true artist. It is not the mere matter that such men create their universe as surely as shipwrecked bits of life run riot and transform themselves on oceanic islands. It is that in this supremely heightened consciousness of genius the mind *demands* expression. The spirit literally cannot remain within itself. It will talk if it talks on paper only to itself, as in the case of Thoreau.

Anxiety, the disease which many psychiatrists seek to excise completely from the human psyche, is here carried up to painful but enormously creative heights. The freedom of genius, its passage beyond the bonds of culture which controls the behavior of the average man, in itself demands the creation of new modes of being. Says Yeats:

Man's life is thought and he despite his terror cannot cease
Ravening through century after century . . .
That he may come
Into the desolation of reality.

Within that desolation, whether he be scientist or poet, man—for this is the nature of his inmost being—will build ever anew. It is not in his nature to do otherwise.

Thoreau, however, presents in his writing an interesting paradox. In his reference to the excessive strain of heightened attention, one might get the impression that creativity was to him a highly conscious exercise that had wriggled into his very fingertips. That he was an intensely perceptive observer there can be no question. Yet, he wrote, in those pre-Freudian, pre-Jungian days of 1852:

I catch myself philosophizing most abstractly when first returning to consciousness in the night or morning. I make the truest observations and distinctions then, when the will is yet wholly asleep and the mind works like a machine without friction. I am conscious of having, in my sleep, transcended the limits of the individual, and made observations and carried on conversations which in my waking hours I can neither recall nor appreciate. As if in sleep our individual fell into the infinite mind, and at the moment of awakening we found ourselves on the confines of the latter.

"It is," he confides in another place, "the material of all things loose and set afloat that makes my sea."

Psychiatrist Lawrence Kubie has speculated that "the creative person is one who in some manner, which today is still accidental, has retained his capacity to use his pre-conscious functions more freely than is true of others who may potentially be equally gifted." While I do not believe that the time will ever come when each man can release his own Shakespeare, I do not doubt that the freedom to create is somehow linked with facility of access to those obscure regions below the conscious mind.

There is, perhaps, a wonderful analogy here between the potential fecundity of life in the universe and those novelties which natural selection in a given era permits to break through the living screen, the biosphere, into reality. Organic opportunity has thus placed sharp limits upon a far greater life potential than is ever permitted to enter the actual world. Yet this other hidden world, a world of possible but nonexistent futures, is a constant accompaniment, a real but wholly latent twin, of the nature in which we have our being. In a strangely similar manner the mental Censor of a too rigidly blocked or distorted unconscious may interfere, not alone with genius, but even with what might be called ordinary productivity.

Just as, in a given situation, the living biological screen may prevent the emergence of a higher form of life, or precipitate its destruction, so in that dark, soundless area of the brain, which parallels the similarly pregnant void of space, much may be barred from creation that exists only as a potentiality. Here again, culturally imposed forms and individual experiences may open or keep permanently closed the doorways of life. The role of purely genetic expression becomes frightfully obscured by the environmental complexities which surround the birth and development of the individual. There is no doubt that clinical studies devoted to creativity, including private interviews with cooperating and contemporary men of genius, offer the prospect of gaining greater insight into those dark alleys and byways out of which stumble at infrequent intervals the Shelleys, the Shakespeares, the Newtons, and the Darwins of our world.

Sometimes they are starved by poverty, self-schooled, sometimes they have known wealth, sometimes they have appeared like comets across an age of violence. Or they have been selfless, they have been beautiful or unlovely of body, they have been rake and puritan. One thing alone they have had in common: thought, music, art, transmissible but unique.

VII

If we, as ordinary educators, whose task—the task Dewey envisioned—is to transmit from these enrichers of life their wisdom to the unformed turbulent future, to transform reflection into action consonant with their thought, then some of their luminosity must encompass our minds; their passion must, in degree, break through our opaque thoughts and descend to us. Whether we will it so or not we play, in another form, the part of the biological screen in the natural world, or the psychological Censor to the individual human mind.

As educators, we play this role in our own culture. In innumerable small ways, if we are rigid, dogmatic, arrogant, we shall be laying stone upon stone, an ugly thing. We shall, for such is our power, give the semblance of necessary reality to a future that need never have been permitted. The educator can be the withholder as well as the giver of life.

I should like, in terminating these remarks, to speak about an experience of my own. I began by offering a case history for your examination, the case history of an

obscure educator who, within the course of a single lifetime has passed from a world of almost primordial il-
literacy and isolation to one which permits wandering
at will among such towering minds as we have been dis-
cussing. In the end, their loneliness has been my loneliness; their poverty I have endured; their wasted days
have been my own. Even their desolate islands, their
deserts, and their forests, have been mine to tread.

Unlike them I cannot speak with tongues, unlike them
I cannot even adequately describe my wanderings. Yet
for a brief interval as a teacher and lecturer I have been
allowed to act as their interpreter and because no man
knows what vibrations he sets in motion in his lifetime, I
am content. Has not St. Paul said that there are many
kinds of voices in the world and none is without sig-
nification?

At a university's opening exercises, in this era of carefully directed advising, in this day of grueling college
board examinations and aptitude tests, I have been permitted just once to cry out to our herded youngsters:
"Wait, forget the Dean of Admissions who, if I came
today in youth before him might not have permitted me
to register, be wary of our dubious advice, step softly
till you have tasted those springs of knowledge which
invite your thirst. Freshmen, sophomores, with the beauti-

53

ful gift of youth upon you, do not be prematurely withered up by us. Are you uncertain about your destiny? Take heart, I, at fifty am still seeking my true calling. I was born a stranger. Perhaps some of you are strangers too." I said this, and much more besides, and was blushing for my impulsive folly, when students I did not know began to invade my office or come up to speak to me on the campus.

I learned in that moment just how much we have lost in our inability to communicate across the generations. I learned how deep, how wrapped in mummy cloth, repressed, long buried, lies in our minds the darkest wound that time has given us. The men of my profession speak frequently of the physical scars of evolution. They mean by this that we carry in our bodies evidence of the long way we have traveled. There is written even in our bones the many passages at arms upon the road. To the student of the past we are as scarred and ragged as old battle flags. We drag with us into the future the tatters of defeat as well as of victory: impulses of deep-buried animal aggressiveness, unconscious mid-brain rivalries that hurl us into senseless accidents upon the road, even as nations, which, after all, are but a few men magnified, similarly destroy themselves upon the even more dangerous road of history.

From the standpoint of the hungry spirit, however, humanity has suffered an even greater wound: the ability of the mind to extend itself across a duration greater than the capacity of mortal flesh to endure. It is part of the burden of all these hungry creative voices that assail us, as it is part of the unsophisticated but equally hungry students who followed me to my office, not because of me, but because of some chord in their minds which I must have momentarily and unconsciously plucked. It is, in brief, the wound of time—that genius of man, which, as Emerson long ago remarked, "is a continuation of the power that made him and that has not done making him."

When man acquired "otherness," when he left the safe confines of the instinctive world of animals, he became conscious of his own mortality. Locked in this evolution-scarred and wounded body was a mind which needed only the stimulus of knowledge to reach across the eons of the past, or to hurl itself upon the future. Has it occurred to us sufficiently that it is part of the continuing growth of this mind that it may *desire* to be lost—lost among whalebones in the farthest seas, in that great book of which Melville, its author, wrote, "a polar wind blows through it," lost among the instinctive villainies of insects in the parched field where Henri Fabre labored, lost with St. Exupéry amidst the crevasses and thin air of the high Andes, down which the first airmail pilots drifted to their deaths. Are these great visions and insights matter for one lifetime that we must needs compress them, safely controlled, into the little rivulet of a single profession at twenty—the powers exorcised, the magnificent torrent siphoned into the safe container of a single life—this mind which, mortal and encased in flesh, would contain the past and seek to devour eternity? "As the dead man is spiritualized . . . ," remarks Thoreau, "so the imagination requires a long range. It is the faculty of the poet to see present things as if also past and future; as if distant or universally significant." The evolutionary wound we bear has been the creation of a thing abstracted out of time yet trapped within it: the mind, by chance distorted, locked into a white-ribbed cage which effervesces into air the moment it approaches wisdom.

These are our students and ourselves, sticks of fragile calcium, little sacks of watery humors that dry away in too much heat, or turn crystalline with cold; no great thing, really, if the thermometer is to be our gauge, or the small clerk stool of a single profession is to measure life. Rather, "What shall be grand in thee," wrote Melville searching his far-flung waters of memory, "must needs be plucked at from the skies, and dived for in the deep, and featured in the unbodied air."

VIII

Not all men possess this stamina, not all sustain such flights of intellect, but each of us should be aware that they exist. It is important that creature comfort does not dull the mind to somnolence. "The more an organism learns," John Dewey remarked in *Experience and Nature*, "the more it has to learn in order to keep itself going." This acceleration, so well documented in the history of civilization, is perceived by Dewey to characterize inflexibly the life of the individual. As an archaeologist, however, gazing from the air upon the faint outlines of the neolithic hill forts still visible upon the English downs or, similarly, upon the monoliths of Stonehenge, or with equal intensity watching a blacksnake glide slowly down the steps of an abandoned Mexican cathedral, I am aware of something else than the geometric extension of power, whether in a civilization or a man.

There comes a time when the thistles spring up over man's ruins with a sense of relief. It is as though the

57

wasting away of power through time had brought with it the retreat of something shadowy and not untouched with evil. The tiny incremental thoughts of men tend to congeal in strange vast fabrics, from gladiatorial coliseums to skyscrapers, and then mutely demand release. In the end the mind rejects the hewn stone and rusting iron it has used as the visible expression of its inner dream. Instead it asks release for new casts at eternity, new opportunities to confine in fanes the uncapturable and elusive gods.

It is one of the true functions of education to teach, in just this figurative way, the pure recompense of observing sunlight and the nodding weed wash over our own individual years and ruins. Joy was there and lingers in the grasses, the black wrong lies forever buried and the tortured mind may seek its peace. Here all is open to the sun. The youthful rebel lies down with his double, the successful man. Or the reverse—who is to judge?

I, who endured the solitude of an Ice Age in my youth, remember now the yellow buttercups of the only picnic I was ever taken on in kindergarten. There are other truths than those contained in laboratory burners, on blackboards, or in test tubes. With the careful suppressions of age the buttercups grow clearer in my memory year by year. I am trying to speak honestly from my own

58

experience. I am trying to say that buttercups, a mastodon tooth, a giant snail, and a rolling Elizabethan line are a part of my own ruins over which the weeds grow tall.

I have not paused there in many years, but the light grows long in retrospect, and I have peace because I am released from pain. I know not how, yet I know also that I have been in some degree created by those lost objects in the grass. We are in truth sculptors in snow, we educators, but, thank God, we are sometimes aided by that wild fitfulness which is called "hazard," "contingency," and the indeterminacy which Dewey labeled "thinking." If the mind is indigenous and integral to nature itself in its unfolding, and operates in nature's ways and under nature's laws, we must seek to understand this creative aspect of nature in its implications for the human mind. I have tried, therefore, to point out that the natural laws of the mind include an emergent novelty with which education has to cope and elaborate for its best and fullest realization. As Thoreau has again anticipated, "[Man's] thought must live with and be inspired with the life of the body."

In Bimini, on the old Spanish Main, a black girl once said to me: "Those as hunts treasure must go alone, at night, and when they find it they have to leave a little of their blood behind them."

59

I have never heard a finer, cleaner estimate of the price of wisdom. I wrote it down at once under a sea lamp, like the belated pirate I was, for the girl had given me unknowingly the latitude and longitude of a treasure—a treasure more valuable than all the aptitude tests of this age.

Bibliography

Arvin, Newton, *Herman Melville: A Critical Biography*, Viking Press, Compass Books Edition, New York, 1957.

Dewey, John, *The Quest for Certainty*, G. P. Putnam's Sons, Capricorn Edition, New York, 1960.

———— *Experience and Nature*, Dover Publications, 2nd Edition, New York, 1958.

Eiseley, Loren, *Darwin's Century*, Doubleday, New York, 1958.

Jarrell, Randall, "On Preparing to Read Kipling," *American Scholar*, vol. 31, pp. 220-235, 1962.

Kubie, Lawrence, *Neurotic Distortion of the Creative Process*, University of Kansas Press, Lawrence, Kansas, 1958.

Newsom, Carroll, *A University President Speaks Out*, Harper & Brothers, New York, 1962.

Olson, Charles, *Call Me Ishmael: A Study of Melville*, Grove Press, New York, 1947.

Petitclerc, Denne, Interview with Robert Hofstadter, *San Francisco Chronicle*, Nov. 4, 1961, p. 4.

Rokeach, Milton, "The Pursuit of the Creative Process," in *The Creative Organization*, edited by Gary Steiner, Free Press, Glencoe, Ill., 1962.

Rostand, Jean, *The Substance of Man*, Doubleday, New York, 1962.

Schneer, Cecil J., *The Search for Order*, Harper & Brothers, New York, 1960.

Thoreau, H. D., *A Writer's Journal*. Selected and edited by Laurence Stapleton, Dover Publications, New York, 1960.

Van Doren, Mark, *Nathaniel Hawthorne: A Critical Biography*, Viking Press, Compass Books Edition, New York, 1957.

About the Author

A noted anthropologist, author, and educator, LOREN EISELEY has served as provost of the University of Pennsylvania and is currently University Professor of Anthropology and the History of Science and chairman of the Department of the History and Philosophy of Science in the Graduate School at the University of Pennsylvania. For the academic year 1961-1962, Dr. Eiseley was in residence at the Institute for Advanced Study in the Behavioral Sciences at Stanford, California.

Born in Lincoln, Nebraska, he was educated at the University of Nebraska and the University of Pennsylvania, where he received his doctorate in 1937.

Dr. Eiseley regularly contributes science articles and essays to popular magazines and is recognized as one of the country's leading writers of non-fiction. His books include *The Immense Journey*, *Darwin's Century*, and *The Firmament of Time*—for which he has received the following honors: The Athenaeum of Philadelphia Literature Award, the Phi Beta Kappa Science Award, the John Burroughs Association Medal, the Lecomte du Noüy Award, and the 1962 Award in Literature at the Philadelphia Arts Festival.